U0111783

大展好書　好書大展
品嘗好書　冠群可期

大展好書　好書大展

品嘗好書　冠群可期

少林傳統功夫漢英對照系列　⑪

Shaolin Traditional Kungfu Series Books　⑪

看 家 拳

（ 一 路 ）

Special Boxing（one routine）

耿 軍 著

Written by Geng Jun

大展出版社有限公司

作者簡介

耿軍（法號釋德君），1968 年 11 月出生於河南省孟州市，係少林寺三十一世皈依弟子。中國武術七段、全國十佳武術教練員、中國少林武術研究會副秘書長、焦作市政協十屆常委、濟南軍區特警部隊特邀武功總教練、洛陽師範學院客座教授、英才教育集團董事長。1989 年創辦孟州少林武術院、2001 年創辦英才雙語學校。先後獲得河南省優秀青年新聞人物、全國優秀武術教育家等榮譽稱號。

1983 年拜在少林寺住持素喜法師和著名武僧素法大師門下學藝，成為大師的關門弟子，後經素法大師引薦，又隨螳螂拳一代宗師李占元、金剛力功于憲華等大師學藝。在中國鄭州國際少林武術節、全國武林精英大賽、全國武術演武大會等比賽中 6 次獲得少林武術冠軍；在中華傳統武術精粹大賽中獲得了象徵少林武術最高榮譽的「達摩杯」一座。他主講示範的 36 集《少林傳統功夫》教學片已由人民體育音像出版社出版發行。他曾多次率團出訪海外，在國際武術界享有較高聲譽。

　　他創辦的孟州少林武術院，現已發展成爲豫北地區最大的以學習文化爲主、以武術爲辦學特色的封閉式、寄宿制學校，是中國十大武術教育基地之一。

Brief Introduction to the Author

Geng Jun〔also named Shidejun in Buddhism〕, born in Mengzhou City of Henan Province, November 1968, is a Bud-dhist disciple of the 31st generation, the 7th section of Chinese Wu shu, national "Shijia" Wu shu coach, Vice Secretary General of China Shaolin Wu shu Research Society, standing committee member of 10th Political Consultative Conference of Jiaozuo City, invited General Kungfu Coach of special police of Jinan Military District, visiting professor of Luoyang Normal University, and Board Chairman of Yingcai Education Group. In 1989, he estab-lished Mengzhou Shaolin Wu shu Institute; in 2001, he estab -lished Yingcai Bilingual School. He has been successively awarded honorable titles of "Excellent Youth News Celebrity of Henan Province" "State Excellent Wu shu Educationalist" etc.

In 1983, he learned Wu shu from Suxi Rabbi, the Abbot of Shaolin Temple, and Grandmaster Sufa, a famous Wu shu monk, and became the last disciple of the

Grandmaster. Then recom‑mended by Grandmaster Sufa, he learned Wu shu from masters such as Li Zhanyuan, great master of mantis boxing, and Yu Xianhua who specializes in Jingangli gong. He won the Shaolin Wu shu champion for 6 times in China Zhengzhou International Wu shu Festival, National Competition of Wu lin Elites, National Wu shu Performance Conference, etc. and one "Damo Trophy" that symbolizes the highest honor of Shaolin Wu shu in Chinese Traditional Wu shu Succinct Competition. 36 volumes teaching VCD of Shaolin Traditional Wu shu has been published and is ‑sued by People´s Sports Audio Visual Publishing House. He has led delegations to visit overseas for many times, enjoying high reputation in the martial art circle of the world.

Mengzhou Shaolin Wu shu Institute, established by him, has developed into the largest enclosed type boarding school of Yubei (north of Henan Province) area, which takes knowledge as primary and Wu shu as distinctiveness, also one of China´s top ten Wu shu education bases.

序　言

中華武術源遠流長，門類繁多。

少林武術源自嵩山少林寺，因寺齊名，是我國拳系中著名的流派之一。少林寺自北魏太和十九年建寺以來，已有一千五百多年的歷史。而少林武術也決不是哪一人哪一僧所獨創，它是歷代僧俗歷經漫長的生活歷程，根據生活所需逐步豐富完善而成。

據少林寺志記載許多少林僧人在出家之前就精通武術或慕少林之名而來或迫於生計或看破紅塵等諸多原因削髮爲僧投奔少林，少林寺歷來倡武，並經常派武僧下山，雲遊四方尋師學藝。還請武林高手到寺，如宋朝的福居禪師曾邀集十八家武林名家到寺切磋技藝，推動了少林武術的發展，使少林武術得諸家之長。

本書作者自幼習武，師承素喜、素法和螳螂拳李占元等多位名家，當年如饑似渴在少林寺研習功夫，曾多次在國內外大賽中獲獎。創辦的孟州少林武術院亦是全國著名的武術院校之一，他示範主講的 36 集《少林傳統功夫》教學 VCD 已由人民體育音像出版社發行。

本套叢書的三十多個少林傳統套路和實戰技法是少

林武術的主要內容，部分還是作者獨到心得，很值得一讀，該書還採用漢英文對照，使外國愛好者無語言障礙，爲少林武術走向世界做出了自己的貢獻，亦是可喜可賀之事。

張耀庭題
甲申秋月

Preface

Chinese Wushu is originated from ancient time and has a long history, it has various styles.

Shaolin Wushu named from the Shaolin Temple of Songshan Mountain, it is one of the famous styles in the Chinese boxing genre. Shaolin temple has more than 1500 years of history since its establishment in the 19th year of North Wei Taihe Dynasty. No one genre of Shaolin Wushu is created solely by any person or monk, but completed gradually by Buddhist monks and common people from generation to generation through long–lasting living course according to the requirements of life. As recording of Record of Shaolin Temple, many Shaolin Buddhist monks had already got a mastery of Wushu before they became a Buddhist monk, they came to Shaolin for tonsure to be a Buddhist monk due to many reasons such as admiring for the name of Shaolin, or by force of life or seeing through thevanity of life. The Shaolin Temple always promotes Wushu and frequently appoints Wushu Buddhist monks to go down the mountain to roam around for searching masters and learning Wushu from them. It also invites

Wushu experts to come to the temple, such as Buddhist monk Fuju of Song Dynasty, it once invited Wushu famous exports of 18 schools to come to the temple to make skill interchange, which promoted the development of Shaolin Wushu and made it absorb advantages of all other schools.

The author learned from many famous exports such as Suxi, Sufa and Li Zhanyuan of Mantis Boxing, he studied Chinese boxing eagerly in Shaolin Temple, and got lots of awards both at home and abroad, he also set up the Mengzhou Shaolin Wushu Institute, which is one of the most famous Wushu institutes around China. He makes demonstration and teaching in the 36 volumes teaching VCD of Shaolin Traditional Wushu, which have been published by Peoples sports Audio Visual publishing house.

There are more than 30 traditional Shaolin routines and practical techniques in this series of books, which are the main content of Shaolin Wushu, and part of which is the original things learned by the author, it is worthy of reading. The series books adopt Chinese and English versions, make foreign fans have no language barrier, and make contribution to Shaolin Wushu going to the world, which is delighting and congratulating thing.

Titled by Zhang Yaoting

目　錄
Contents

看家拳（一路）

説　明

（一）為了表述清楚，以圖像和文字對動作作了分解說明，練習時應力求連貫銜接。

（二）在文字說明中，除特別說明外，不論先寫或後寫身體的某一部分，各運動部位都要求協調活動、連貫銜接，切勿先後割裂。

（三）動作方向轉變以人體為準，標明前後左右。

（四）圖上的線條是表明這一動作到下一動作經過的線路及部位。左手、左腳及左轉均為虛線（┈┈►）；右手、右腳及右轉均為實線（──►）。

Instructions

(i) In order to explain clearly figures and words are used to describe the actions in multi steps. Try to keep coherent when exercising.

(ii) In the word instruction, unless special instruction, each action part of the body shall act harmoniously and join coherently no matter it is written first or last, please do not separate the actions.

(iii) The action direction shall be turned taking body as standard, which is marked with front, back, left or right.

(iv) The line in the figure shows the route and position from this action to the next action. The left hand, left foot and turn left are all showed in broken line (⎯⎯►) ; the right hand, right foot and turn right are all showed in real line (⎯⎯►) .

基本步型與基本手型
Basic stances and Basic hand forms

基本步型與基本手型

圖 1

圖 2

圖 3

圖 4

圖 5

圖 6

圖 7

圖 8

圖 9

圖 10

圖 11

圖 12

基本步型與基本手型

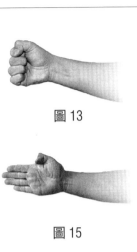

圖 13

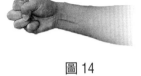

圖 14

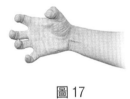

圖 15

圖 16

圖 17

圖 18

圖 19

圖 20

圖 21

基本步型

　　少林武術中常見的步型有：弓步、馬步、仆步、虛步、歇步、坐盤步、丁步、併步、七星步、跪步、高虛步、翹腳步 12 種。

　　弓步：俗稱弓箭步。兩腿前後站立，兩腳相距本人腳長的 4～5 倍；前腿屈至大腿接近水平，腳尖微內扣不超過 5°；後腿伸膝挺直，腳掌內扣 45°。（圖 1）

　　馬步：俗稱騎馬步。兩腳開立，相距本人腳長的 3～3.5 倍，兩腳尖朝前；屈膝下蹲大腿接近水平，膝蓋與兩腳尖上下成一條線。（圖 2）

　　仆步：俗稱單叉，一腿屈膝全蹲，大腿貼緊小腿，膝微外展，另一腿直伸平仆接近地面，腳掌扣緊與小腿成 90°夾角。（圖 3）

　　虛步：又稱寒雞步。兩腳前後站立，前後相距本人腳長的 2 倍；重心移至後腿，後腿屈膝下蹲至大腿接近水平，腳掌外擺 45°；前腿腳尖點地，兩膝相距 10 公分。（圖 4）

　　歇步：兩腿左右交叉，靠近全蹲；前腳全腳掌著地，腳尖外展，後腳腳前掌著地，臀部微坐於後腿小腿上。（圖 5）

　　坐盤步：在歇步的形狀下，坐於地上，後腿的大小腿外側和腳背均著地。（圖 6）

基本步型與基本手型

　　丁步：兩腿併立，屈膝下蹲，大腿接近水平，一腳尖點地靠近另一腳內側腳窩處。（圖7）

　　併步：兩腿併立，屈膝下蹲，大腿接近水平。（圖8）

　　七星步：七星步是少林七星拳和大洪拳中獨有的步型。一腳內側腳窩內扣於另一腳腳尖，兩腿屈膝下蹲，接近水平。（圖9）

　　跪步：又稱小蹬山步。兩腳前後站立，相距本人腳長的2.5倍，前腿屈膝下蹲，後腿下跪，接近地面，後腳腳跟離地。（圖10）

　　高虛步：又稱高點步。兩腳前後站立，重心後移，後腿腳尖外擺45°，前腿腳尖點地，兩腳尖相距一腳距離。（圖11）

　　翹腳步：在七星螳螂拳中又稱七星步，兩腿前後站立，相距本人腳長的1.5倍，後腳尖外擺45°，屈膝下蹲，前腿直伸，腳跟著地，腳尖微內扣。（圖12）

基本手型

　　少林武術中常見的手型有拳、掌、鉤3種。

　　拳：

　　分為平拳和透心拳。

　　平拳：平拳是武術中較普遍的一種拳型，又稱方拳。四指屈向手心握緊，拇指橫屈扣緊食指。（圖

13）

　　透心拳：此拳主要用於打擊心窩處，故名。四指併攏捲握，中指突出拳面，拇指扣緊抵壓中指梢節處。（圖14）

　　掌：

　　分為柳葉掌、八字掌、虎爪掌、鷹爪掌、鉗指掌。

　　柳葉掌：四指併立，拇指內扣。（圖15）

　　八字掌：四指併立，拇指張開。（圖16）

　　虎爪掌：五指分開，彎曲如鉤，形同虎爪。（圖17）

　　鷹爪掌：又稱鎖喉手，拇指內扣，小指和無名指彎曲扣於掌心處，食指和中指分開內扣。（圖18）

　　鉗指掌：五指分開，掌心內含。（圖19）

　　鉤：

　　分為鉤手和螳螂鉤。

　　鉤手：屈腕，五指自然內合，指尖相攏。此鉤使用較廣，武術中提到的鉤均為此鉤。（圖20）

　　螳螂鉤：又稱螳螂爪，屈腕成腕部上凸，無名指、小指屈指內握，食指、中指內扣，拇指梢端按貼於食指中節。（圖21）

Basic stances

基本步型與基本手型

Usual stances in Shaolin Wushu are: bow stance, horse stance, crouch stance, empty stance, rest stance, cross – legged sitting, T – stance, feet – together stance, seven – star stance, kneel stance, high empty stance, and toes – raising stance, these twelve kinds.

Bow stance: commonly named bow – and – arrow stance. Two feet stand in tandem, the distance between two feet is about four or five times of length of one´s foot; the front leg bends to the extent of the thigh nearly horizontal with toes slightly turned inward by less than 5°; the back leg stretches straight with the sole turned inward by 45°. (Figure 1)

Horse stance: commonly named riding step. two feet stand apart, the distance between two feet is 3~3.5 times of length of one´s foot, with tiptoes turned forward; bend knees to squat downward, with thighs nearly horizontal, knees and two tiptoes in line. (Figure 2)

Crouch stance: commonly named single split. Bend the knee of one leg and squat entirely with thigh very close to lower leg and knee outspread slightly; straighten the other leg and crouch horizontally close to floor, keep the sole turned inward and forming an included angle of 90° with lower leg. (Figure 3)

Empty stance: also named cold – chicken stance. Two feet stand in tandem, the distance between two feet is 2 times of

length of one´s foot; transfer the barycenter to back leg, bend the knee of the back leg and squat downward to the extent of the thigh nearly horizontal, with the sole turned outward by 45°; keep the tiptoe of front leg on the ground, with distance between two knees of 10cm. (Figure 4)

Rest stance: cross the two legs at left and right, keep them close and entirely squat; keep the whole sole of the front foot on the ground with tiptoes turned outward, the front sole of the back foot on the ground, and buttocks slightly seated on the lower leg of the back leg. (Figure 5)

Cross – legged sitting: in the posture of rest stance, sit on the ground, with the outer sides of the thigh and lower leg of the back leg and instep on the ground. (Figure 6)

T – stance: two legs stand with feet together, bend knees and squat to the extent of the thighs nearly horizontal, with one tiptoe on the ground and close to inner side of the fossa of the other foot. (Figure 7)

Feet – together stance: two legs stand with feet together, bend knees and squat to the extent of the thigh nearly horizontal. (Figure 8)

Seven – star stance: Seven – star step is a unique step form in Shaolin Seven – star Boxing and Major Flood Boxing. Keep the inner side of the fossa of one foot turned inward onto tiptoe of the other foot, bend two knees and squat nearly horizontal. (Figure 9)

Kneel stance: also named small mountaineering stance. Two feet stand in tandem, the distance between two feet is 2.5

times of length of one´s foot, bend knee of the front leg and squat, kneel the back leg close to the floor, with the heel of back foot off the floor. (Figure 10)

High empty stance: also named high point stance. Two feet stand in tandem. Transfer the barycenter backward, turn the tiptoe of the back leg outward by 45°, with tiptoe of front leg on the ground, and the distance between two tiptoes is length of one foot. (Figure 11)

Toes –raising stance: also named seven –star stance in Seven –star Mantis Boxing. Two legs stand in tandem, and the distance between two legs is 1.5 times of length of one´s foot. Keep the tiptoe of back leg turned outward by 45°, bend knees and squat, straighten the front leg with heel on the ground and tiptoe turned inward slightly. (Figure 12)

Basic hand forms

Usual hand forms in Shaolin Wushu are: fist, palm and hook, these three kinds.

Fist: classified into straight fist and heart–penetrating fist.

Flat fist: a rather common fist form in Wushu, also named square fist. Hold the four fingers tightly toward the palm, and horizontally bend the thumb to button up the fore finger. (Figure 13)

Heart –penetrating fist: mainly used for striking the heart part. Put four fingers together and coil –hold them, the middle finger thrusts out the striking surface of the fist, the thumb

buttons up and presses the end and joint of the middle finger. (Figure 14)

Palm: classified into willow leaf palm, splay palm, tiger's claw palm, eagle's claw palm, fingers clamping palm.

Willow leaf palm: palm with four fingers up and thumb turned inward. (Figure 15)

Eight–shape palm: palm with four fingers up and thumb splay. (Figure 16)

Tiger's claw palm: palm with five fingers apart, bent as hook and like tiger's claw. (Figure 17)

Eagle's claw palm: also named throat locking hand, with the thumb turned inward, the little finger and middle finger turned onto palm, fore finger and middle finger apart and turned inward. (Figure 18)

Fingers clamp palm: palm with five fingers apart and palm drawn in. (Figure 19)

Hook: classified into hook hand and mantis hook.

Hook hand: bend the wrist, five fingers drawn in naturally with fingertips together. This hook is used in wide range, the hook mentioned in Wushu refers to this. (Figure 20)

Mantis hook: also named mantis' claw, bend wrist into wrist bulge upward, the ring finger and little finger bend to hold inward, with fore finger and fore middle finger turned inward and end of thumb pressed on the middle joint of the fore finger. (Figure 21)

看家拳（一路）套路簡介

Brief Introduction to the Routine Special Boxing（one routine）

　　少林看家拳是宋代福居禪師為防止有些寺僧學藝不精，出寺後有辱少林聲譽，便召集寺內武僧高手研究提煉了少林武術的精華招式，傳授給 26 名武僧，設 13 道關卡，每道關卡由兩名武僧把守，規定任何僧俗弟子想出山，必須打敗這守關武僧，方可出師下山，否則將受跪香的懲罰，並苦苦修練。這守關的招式漸漸形成了套路——少林十三路看家拳。

　　1906 年少林弟子貞方把一份少林看家拳譜帶回山東故鄉，在 1936 年把該套路拳譜傳給了少林寺第二十九世著名武僧貞秋的弟子素法，素法研究五十餘年，1986 年又傳給了關門弟子耿軍。

　　Shaolin special boxing is an essential routine, originated to prevent the monk of the temple who didn´t learn the skill well and disgraced the Shaolin´s prestige after they exited the temple by the Buddhist monk Fuju at Song Dynasty. He called together the proficient Wushu monks in the temple to study and abstract the essential postures of the Shaolin Wushu, and taught it to 26 Wushu monks, then set 13 toll-gates with each toll-gates

guarded by two Wushu monks, and stipulated that any monk or common disciple who wanted to go out from the mountain must beat the monks who guarded the toll-gates at first, otherwise, he must accept the punishment of joss sticks kneeling and make more efforts to learn skills. These postures which were used for guarding the toll-gates gradually formed a Taolu——The Shaolin Special Boxing of 13 routines.

In 1906, Zhenfang, one Shaolin disciple, carried a copy of the book of the Shaolin Special Boxing back to his hometown Shandong Province and passed it to Sufa who is the disciple of the 29th generation notable Wushu monk Zhenqiu of the Shaolin Temple in 1936. Sufa studied it for more than 50 years, and passed it to his last disciple Geng Jun.

看家拳（一路）套路動作名稱
Action Names of Routine
Special Boxing（one routine）

第一段　Section One

1. 預備勢　Preparatory posture
2. 運掌　Move the palms
3. 舉鼎　Lift the vessel
4. 兩手托平　Both hands extend levelly
5. 上步玉柱　Step forward into jade-column
6. 跳起拍打　Jump and slap
7. 丁步架打　Parry and punch in T- stance
8. 單踢　Single kick
9. 弓步沖拳　Thrust fist in bow stance
10. 裏合腿　Inward slap crescent kick
11. 拗式單鞭　Twist style single whip
12. 旋風腳　Whirlwind kick
13. 騎馬勢　Horse-riding posture

第二段　Section Two

14. 霸王舉鼎　The overlord lifts the vessel

15. 提腿磕膝　Lift leg and knock knee

16. 右踹腿　Right side heel kick

17. 坐蓮護耳掌　Ear-guarding palm with lotus seat

18. 擺蓮腿　Lotus kick

19. 洪門射雁　Shoot wild goose at Hongmen

20. 按窩呂夫　Nest-pressing Lvfu

21. 肘腿　Elbow and kick

22. 仆步伏虎　Tame the tiger in crouch stance

23. 前掃腿　Sweep leg forward

24. 騎馬勢　Horse-riding posture

25. 匡捶　Parry with hammer

26. 弓步沖拳　Thrust fist in bow stance

27. 彈腿沖拳　Snap kick and thrust fist

28. 翻身護肩掌　Turn over and guard shoulder with palm

29. 金龍抱玉柱　Golden dragon embraces jade–column

30. 童子拜佛　The boy worships Buddha

第三段　Section Three

31. 野馬分鬃　Part the wild horse´s mane

32. 八步趕蟬　Chase cicada in eight steps

33. 二起腳　Jumping kick twice

34. 旋風腿　Whirlwind kick

35. 代腿飛擺蓮　Flying lotus kick with additional leg

36. 洪門射雁　Shoot wild goose at Hongmen
37. 左右梅花手　Left and right plumb-blossom hand
38. 虛步亮掌　Flash palm in empty stance
39. 謝步請勢　Invitation posture with backward step
40. 收勢　Closing form

看家拳（一路）套路動作名稱

看家拳（一路）套路動作圖解

Action Illustrtion of Routine
Special Boxing（one routine）

圖1

第一段　Section One

1. 預備勢　Preparatory posture

　　兩腳併立；兩手自然下垂，五指併攏，貼於體側；目視前方。（圖1）

　　要點：身體正立，挺胸塌腰，頭正頸直。

看家拳（一路）套路動作圖解

Stand upright with feet together, and the hands drop naturally with the fingers together and close to both sides of the body. Eyes look forward.（Figure 1）

Key points: the body stands upright. Lift the chest and lower waist downward, with head being correctitude and neck straight.

圖 2

2. 運掌　Move the palms

（1）接上勢。左腳向左開步，與肩同寬；同時，兩掌從身體兩側向上緩緩抬起，兩掌心均向下，高與肩平；目視前方。（圖 2）

（1）Follow the above posture, the left foot moves step leftward, shoulder-width apart. Meanwhile, both palms lift up slowly from both sides of the body, with both palms down, at the shoulder height. Eyes look forward.（Figure 2）

看家拳（一路）套路動作圖解

圖 3

(2) 上動不停。兩掌內旋，成掌心向上並向胸前合攏，兩臂伸直，兩掌指均向前，高與肩平。（圖 3）

(2) Keep the above action, both palms turn inward into its centers upward and meeting in front of the chest, both arms extend straight with both palm fingers forward in height at same level with the shoulder.（Figure 3）

圖 4

　　⑶ 上動不停。兩臂屈肘，兩掌緩緩收於胸前，高與肩平，兩掌心均向裏，十指相對。（圖 4）

　　(3) Keep the above action, bend the elbows, and draw back both palms slowly in front of the chest at the same level with the shoulder. Both palms inward and ten fingers opposite.（Figure 4）

圖 5

⑷上動不停。兩掌下翻並緩緩向下按掌，置於小
腹前，兩掌心均向下，十指相對；目視前方。（圖 5）

要點：精神貫注，心無雜念，以意領氣，氣沉丹
田。

⑷ Keep the above action, turn both palms down－ward and
press them downward slowly to set it in front of the lower
abdomen, Both palms are downwardm, with ten fingers opposite.
Eyes look forward.（Figure 5）

Key points: keep preoccupant with no distracting thoughts,
take thought to lead qi and make qi settle in the Dantian.

圖6

3. 舉鼎　Lift the vessel

接上勢。兩掌內翻，經胸前向上托掌，至面前時翻掌上托於頭頂上方，兩掌心均向上，十指相對；目視兩掌指尖。（圖6）

Follow the above posture, both palms turn inward to raise the palms upward through the front of the chest and turn the palms to support them above the head top when in front of the faces. Both the palms are upward with 10 fingers opposite. Eyes look at fingertips of both palms.（Figure 6）

圖 7

4. 兩手托平　Both hands extend levelly

（1）接上勢。抬右腳震腳，隨即左腳向前上半步，腳尖點地成左虛步；同時，兩掌從身體兩側下落並收於腰間，掌心向上，掌指向前；目視前方。（圖 7）

（1）Follow the above posture, lift the right foot and stamp it, then the left foot steps half a step forward, with the tiptoes on floor forming left empty stance. Meanwhile, both palms fall from both sides of the body and rest on the waist, with the palm up and fingers forward. Eyes look forward.（Figure 7）

圖 8

(2) 上動不停。兩掌從腰間向前穿掌，兩臂微屈，掌心向上，掌指向前，高與肩平；目視前方。（圖 8）

要點：右腳震腳有力，抖肩發力向前穿掌，力達十指尖。

(2) Keep the above action, thread both palms for-ward from the waist, with both arms bent slightly, palm up and fingers forward, in height as shoulder. Eyes look forward.〔Figure 8〕

Key points: right foot stamp shall be forceful; shake shoulder to send force to thread the palm forward, and the force shall reach the ten fingertips.

圖 9

5. 上步玉柱 Step forward into jade – column

（1）接上勢。左腳向前上步，身體起立，重心移至兩腿間；同時，兩掌從胸前向下、向後擺掌於兩胯側，兩掌心均向前，掌指均向下。（圖 9）

（1）Follow the above posture, left foot steps forward. Stand up to move the barycenter to between the two legs. Meanwhile, swing both palms down and backward to both sides of the hips. Keep both palms forward, and the fingers downward. 〔Figure 9〕

圖 10

　　(2) 上動不停。右腳向前上一步；同時，雙手從身體兩側直臂向上舉於頭兩側上方，掌指向上，掌心相對。（圖 10）

　　(2) Keep the above action, the right foot takes a step forward. Meanwhile both hands lift with the arms straight to upper of the both sides of head from both sides of the body, with fingers up and palms opposite.（Figure 10）

看家拳（一路）套路動作圖解

圖11

（3）上動不停。左腳向前併步；同時，兩掌經胸前下按於兩胯側，兩掌心均向下，掌指斜向前，肘微屈；目視左方。（圖11）

要點：上步與按掌要協調一致。

(3) Keep the above action, move the left foot forward to bring feet together. Meanwhile both palms press down at both sides of the hips through the front of chest, keep both palms downward, the fingers forward aslant and the elbows slightly bent. Eyes look leftward.〔Figure 11〕

Key points: stepping forward and pressing the palms down shall be in harmony and consistent.

圖 12

6. 跳起拍打　Jump and slap

（1）接上勢。左腿獨立，右膝提起，腳尖內扣；同時，右手向下拍擊右膝蓋，掌心貼於右膝上；左掌變拳抱於腰間，拳心向上；目視右掌。（圖12）

（1）Follow the above posture, stands on the left leg, lift the right knee and buckle inward the tiptoe. Meanwhile the right hand slaps the right knee downward with the palm close to right knee. Change the left palm into fist and hold it on the waist, with the fist-palm up. Eyes look at the right palm.（Figure 12）

圖 13

（2）上動不停。左腳蹬地跳起，右腳落地獨立；同時，左拳變掌，向下拍擊左膝，掌心落於左膝蓋上；右掌變拳抱於腰間，拳心向上；目視左掌。（圖 13）

要點：跳步要輕靈敏捷，與拍掌協調一致。

(2) Keep the above action, the left foot jumps from floor and right foot falls to the ground to stand on one leg. Meanwhile, change the left fist into palm to slap the left knee downward, with the palm falling on left knee. Change the right palm into fist and hold the fist on the waist, with the fist–palm up. Eyes look at the left palm.（Figure 13）

Key points: jump shall be light and agile, in harmony and consistent with the palm slapping.

圖 14

7. 丁步架打　Parry and punch in T‑stance

（1）接上勢。左腳下落，腳尖點地，身體下蹲成左丁步；同時，左掌變拳，兩拳抱於左腰間，左拳心向上，右拳心向裏；目視兩拳。（圖 14）

（1）Follow the above posture, the left foot lands with the tiptoes on floor, squat the body into left T‑stance. Meanwhile, change the left palm into fist, hold both fists on the left waist. Keep the left fist‑palm up and the right one inward. Eyes look at both fists.（Figure 14）

圖 15

（2）上動不停。左拳向左側平沖，拳心向下，拳眼向前，高與肩平；右拳經胸前上架於頭前上方，拳心斜向上；目視左方。（圖 15）

(2) Keep the above action, horizontally punch the left fist to the left side, with the fist–palm down and fist–hole forward at the shoulders height. Parry the right fist to up front of head through the front of chest, with the fist–palm up aslant. Eyes look leftward.（Figure 15）

看
家
拳
（
一
路
）

圖 16

8. 單踢　Single kick

接上勢。身體左轉 90°，右腿獨立腳尖裏扣，左腿
提起向前彈踢；同時，兩拳收抱於腰間，拳心均向
上；目視前方。（圖 16）

要點：轉身與彈踢要同時進行，力達腳背。

Follow the above posture, turn the body 90° to the left.
Stand on the right leg with toes turned inward, and the left leg
lifts to kick forward. Meanwhile, draw back and hold both fists
on the waist, with both fist –palms up. Eyes look forward.
（Figure 16）

Key points: turning the body and kicking shall be done at
the same time, with the force reaching the instep.

圖 17

9. 弓步沖拳　Thrust fist in bow stance

（1）接上勢。身體右轉 90°，左腳向左落地成馬步；同時，左拳變掌外摟，置於左膝上方，掌心向下，掌指向右；目視左方。（圖 17）

（1）Follow the above posture, turn the body 90° to the right. The left foot falls leftward to the ground into horse stance. Meanwhile, change the left fist into palm and grab the palm outward, and place it above the left knee, with the palm down and fingers rightward. Eyes look leftward.（Figure 17）

看
家
拳
（
一
路
）

圖 18

　　(2) 上動不停。身體左轉 90°，重心前移成左弓步；同時，左掌繼續外摟變拳抱於腰間，拳心向上；右拳隨身向前平沖，拳心向下，拳眼向裏，高與肩平；目視右拳。（圖 18）

　　要點：蹬腿、擰腰、抖肩發力，力達拳面。

(2)Keep the above action, turn the body 90° to the left, shift the barycenter forward into left bow stance. Meanwhile the left palm continues to grab outward, changes into fist and holds on the waist, with the fist –palm up. The right fist thrusts horizontally forward with body turn, with fist –palm down and fist –hole inward at the shoulders height. Eyes look at the right fist.（Figure 18）

Key points: heel kick, twist waist and shake the shoulder to apply force that shall reach the fist–face.

圖 19

10. 裏合腿　Inward slap crescent kick

（1）接上勢。身體起立，略向右轉；同時，右拳收抱於腰間，拳心向上；目視前方。（圖 19）

（1）Follow the above posture, stand up and turn the body slightly to the right. Meanwhile, draw back and hold the right fist on the waist, with the fist–palm up. Eyes look forward.（Figure 19）

圖 20

(2) 上動不停。左腿獨立，右腿抬起由外向裏合
踢；同時，左拳變掌，擊拍右腳內側；目視右腳。
（圖 20）

要點：右腿抬腿要高，迅猛有力，左掌擊響力點
準確，清脆響亮。

(2) Keep the above action, stand on the left leg, raise and
swing the right leg from outward to inward. Meanwhile, change
the left fist into palm to slap the inner side of the right foot. Eyes
look at the right foot.（Figure 20）

Key points: raise the right leg highly, quickly and forcefully,
the clapping point of left palm shall be accurate and sounds
clearly.

看家拳（一路）

圖 21

11. 拗式單鞭　Twist style single whip

接上勢。身體微向右轉，右腳向前落地成右弓步；同時，兩掌交叉於胸前，並分別向身體前後推掌，左掌在前，右掌在後，兩掌指均向上，高與肩平；目視前方。（圖 21）

要點：弓步與推掌同時完成，兩掌先合後分驟然發力，力達兩掌根。

看家拳（一路）套路動作圖解

Follow the above posture, turn the body slightly to the right. The right foot lands to the ground forward into right bow stance. Meanwhile, cross the two palms in front of chest and push them forward and backward of body respectively, with the left palm in front and right palm at back. Keep the fingers upward at the shoulders height. Eyes look forward.（Figure 21）

Key points: bow stance and palm pushing shall be finished simultaneously, the two palms join first and depart then, to exert force suddenly, and the force shall reach the bases of both palms.

圖 22

12. 旋風腳　Whirlwind kick

（1）接上勢。身體左轉 90°，重心左移成馬步；同時，左掌變拳，隨身向左、向下置於小腹前，拳心向下；右掌變拳，隨身向上置於頭上方，拳心向後。（圖 22）

（1）Follow the above posture, turn the body 90° to the left Shift the barycenter leftward into horse stance. Meanwhile, the left palm changes into fist to move leftward and downward in front of lower abdomen, with fist－palm down; change the right palm into fist, and put it ward above the head with body, with the fist－palm backward.（Figure 22）

圖 23

(2) 上動不停。左腿提膝，隨即右腳蹬地跳起，身
體騰空左轉 180°，在空中右腿裏合；同時，左掌向裏
擊拍右腳掌；目視右腳。（圖 23）

要點：身體騰空要高，左掌擊響力點準確，聲音清
脆，整個動作快速連貫。

(2) Keep the above action, the left knee lifts, then the right
foot kicks the ground to jump up, the body turns 180° to the left
in the air, and swing the right leg inward in the air. At the same
time, the left palm slaps the right sole of the foot inward. Eyes
look at the right foot.（Figure 23）

圖 24

13. 騎馬勢 Horse - riding posture

（1）接上勢。身體繼續左轉 180°，左右腳先後落地成馬步；同時，兩手變拳，屈肘合於胸前並齊，兩拳心均向裏，拳面均向上，高與肩平；目視前方。（圖24、圖 24 附圖）

圖 24 附圖

(1) Follow the above posture, the body continues to turn 180° to the left. The left and right foot lands to the ground in order into horse stance. Meanwhile, change both hands into fists, bend the elbows and fold them in front of chest tidily, with both fist-palms inward, fist-planes of up at the shoulders height. Eyes look forward.（Figure 24, Attached figure 24）

看家拳（一路）

圖 25

(2)上動不停。兩拳自胸前分別向身體兩側平沖，
兩虎口均向前，拳心均向下，高與肩平；目視左方。
（圖 25）

看家拳（一路）套路動作圖解

(2) Keep the above action, both fists thrust horizontally from the front of chest to both sides of the body respectively, with both parts of hand between thumb and index finger forward, and fist –palms downward at the shoulders height. Eyes look leftward.（Figure 25）

圖 26

第二段　Section Two

14. 霸王舉鼎　The overlord lifts the vessel

接上勢。右拳向裏經胸前下按於腹前，拳心向下，拳眼向裏；同時，左拳向裏經胸前上架拳於頭前上方，拳眼向下，拳心向前；目視右拳。（圖 26、圖 26 附圖）

圖 26 附圖

Follow the above posture, the right fist moves inward to press down in front of abdomen by front of chest, with the fist-palm down and fist-hole inward.

Meanwhile, left fist moves inward by front of chest to parry upward to upfront of the head, with fist-hole down and fist-palm forward. Eyes look at the right fist.（Figure 26, Attached figure 26）

圖 27

15. 提腿磕膝　Lift leg and knock knee

接上勢。身體微向左傾，左腿起立，右膝提起；同時，兩拳向右膝兩側砸拳，兩拳眼相對，兩拳心相對，拳眼向上；目視右膝。（圖 27）

要點：提膝要含胸圓背，兩拳下砸快捷有力。

Follow the above posture, the body slants slightly leftward. The left leg stand up, and the right knee lifts. Meanwhile, both fists smash to both sides of right knee, with both fist –palms opposite and fist –hole upward. Eyes look at the right knee. （Figure 27）

Key points: lift knee with the chest slightly drawn in and round back, both fists smash down speedily and forcefully.

圖 28

16. 右踹腿　Right side heel kick

接上勢。身體左傾，右腳不落地直接向右側踹出；目視右腳。（圖 28）

要點：身體左傾接近水平，右腿踹腿要高，力達腳掌。

Follow the above posture, incline the body to left, right foot directly kicks out to right side without stepping on floor. Eyes look at the right foot.（Figure 28）

Key points: incline the body to left near horizontally, the right side heel kick shall be high, with the force reaching sole of the foot.

圖 29

17. 坐蓮護耳掌
Ear‑guarding palm with lotus seat

(1) 接上勢。右腳向下落地，重心移至兩腿間；同時，兩拳變掌，在胸前合擊掌，兩臂微屈，右掌指向前，左掌指向上；目視前方。（圖 29、圖 29 附圖）

圖 29 附圖

(1) Follow the above posture, the right foot lands to the ground, and move the barycenter to between the two legs. Meanwhile both fists change into palm and jointly slap in front of chest.（Figure 29, Attached figure 29）

圖 30

　　(2) 上動不停。左腳向右腿後插步，身體下蹲成歇步；同時，兩掌經胸前向下分掌，並向上、向裏擺掌於兩耳側，十指相對，兩掌心均向前；目視前方。（圖 30、圖 30 附圖）

　　要點：蹲歇步要輕靈快捷，與護耳掌協調完成。

圖 30 附圖

(2) Keep the above action, left foot inserts step at back of right leg, body squats down into rest stance. Meanwhile, both palms separate downward by front of chest, and swing upward and inward at sides of ears, with ten fingers opposite and both palms forward. Eyes look forward.（Figure 30, Attached figure 30）

Key points: squatting rest stance shall be light and agile, finished in harmony with ear-quarding palm.

圖 31

18. 擺蓮腿　Lotus kick

接上勢。身體起立，左腿獨立，右腿抬起由裏向外擺腿；同時，左右掌依次拍擊右腳面；目視前方。（圖 31）

要點：右腿外擺迅速有力，兩掌擊響力點準確，聲音清脆。

Follow the above posture, stand up and stand on the left leg, and the right leg lifts to swing from inward to outward. Meanwhile, left and right palm slaps the right instep in order. Eyes look forward.（Figure 31）

Key points: right leg swinging outward shall be fast and forceful; slapping point of both palms shall be accurate and the clap shall sound clearly.

圖 32

19. 洪門射雁　Shoot wild goose at Hongmen

(1) 接上勢。右腳向右落地，身體下蹲成馬步；同時，左掌抱於腰間，掌心向上，掌指向前；右掌向下、向外畫掌並向裏摟手，掌心向下，掌指向左置於身前；目視右掌。（圖32、圖32附圖）

圖 32 附圖

(1) Follow the above posture, right foot falls to the ground rightward, body squats down into horse stance. Meanwhile, hold the left palm on the waist, with palm up and fingers forward. The right palm swings down and outward and grabs inward, with palm down and fingers leftward, and place the right palm in front of bldy. Eyes look at the right palm. ﹙ Figure 32, Attached figure 32 ﹚

圖33

（2）上動不停。身體略向右轉成右弓步；同時，右掌摟抓變拳收抱於腰間，拳心向上；左掌向左平推掌，掌心向外，掌指向上；目視左方。（圖33）

要點：以腰催肩、以肩帶肘推掌，力達掌根。

（2）Keep the above action, body turns slightly to the right into right bow stance. Meanwhile, right palm grabs into fist and draws back to the waist, with fist–palm up, left palm pushes horizontally to left, with palm outward and fingers up. Eyes look leftward.（Figure 33）

Key points: take waist to force shoulder, and shoulder brings elbow to push palm, with force reaching base of the palm.

看家拳（一路）

圖 34

20. 按窩呂夫　Nest‐pressing Lvfu

（1）接上勢。身體略向右轉；同時，右拳變掌，兩掌一起前伸按掌，左臂微屈，右掌在前，左掌在後，兩掌心均向下，高與肩平；目視前方。（圖 34、圖 34附圖）

看家拳（一路）套路動作圖解

圖 34 附圖

(1) Follow the above posture, turn the body slightly to right. Meanwhile, change the right fist into palm, stretch both palms forward together and press them, and bend the left arm slightly, with right palm in front and left palm at back. Keey both palms downward at the shoulders height. Eyes look forward.（Figure 34, Attached figure 34）

圖 35

(2)上動不停。重心後移，右腳收回腳尖點地，身
體後坐成右虛步；同時，兩掌向裏、向下按掌，收回
胸前再翻腕向前擺掌，右掌在前，高與肩平，左掌在
後，附於右肘內側，兩掌均斜向前，掌指均向上；目
視前方。（圖 35）

(2) Keep the above action, shift the barycenter backward,
draw back the right foot with toes on floor, with the body
slightly drawn in into right empty stance. Meanwhile, press both
palms inward and downward, draw them back in front of chest
and turn wrists to swing palms forward, with the right palm in
front at the shoulders height and left palm at back adhering to
inner side of right elbow. Keep both palms inclined forward,
fingers up. Eyes look forward.（Figure 35）

圖 36

21. 肘腿　Elbow and kick

（1）接上勢。身體起立，右腳向前上一小步踏實；同時，左掌收於胸前，掌心向右，掌指向上；右掌收於右肩前，掌指向後，掌心向上；目視前方。（圖36）

（1）Follow the above posture, stand up, right foot steps a small step forward firmly. Meanwhile, draw back the left palm in front of chest, with palm rightward and palm fingers up; draw back the right palm in front of right shoulder, with palm fingers backward and palm up. Eyes look forward.（Figure 36）

圖37

(2) 上動不停。右腿屈膝獨立，左腿以腳和腳外側擦地向前搓踢，腳尖向左上方；同時，兩掌向左後方劈掌，置於左胯側，右掌心向上，掌指向外；左掌心向裏，掌指向後；目視左腳。（圖37）

要點：整個動作要連貫協調，擰腰發勁，快速有力。

看家拳（一路）套路動作圖解

(2) Keep the above action, stand on the right leg with the knee bent, the left leg kicks forward with the shuffling floor, keep the tiptoe left upward. Meanwhile, hack both palms left backward, and place them at side of left hip. Keep the right palm up and fingers outward; the left palm inward and fingers backward. Eyes look at the left foot. ﹝ Figure 37 ﹞

Key points: the whole action shall be harmonic and consistent, waist twisting and force giving out are fast and forceful.

圖 38

22. 仆步伏虎
Tame the tiger in crouch stance

（1）接上勢。左腳向前落地，身體右轉 90°；同時，兩臂隨身擺於身體左後方。（圖 38）

（1）Follow the above posture, left foot lands forward to the ground, and the body turns 90° to the right. Meanwhile, both arms swing left backward with the body.（Figure 38）

圖 39

(2)上動不停。兩腳蹬地跳起，身體騰空右轉180°；同時，兩掌隨身擺舉於頭兩側上方，掌心向前，掌指相對。（圖 39）

(2) Keep the above action, both feet press against floor to jump, the body turn 180° to the right in the air. Meanwhile, swing and lift both palms above both sides of head, with palm forward and fingers opposite.（Figure 39）

看家拳（一路）

圖40

（3）上動不停。右腳落地，左腳向左鏟步平仆成左仆步；同時，左掌經胸前下按於襠前，掌心向下，掌指向右；右掌翻掌上架於頭右側上方，掌心向上，掌指向左；目視左方。（圖40、圖40附圖）

要點：轉身迅速，跳步輕靈，落步穩健，整個動作連貫協調。

圖 40 附圖

(3) Keep the above action, the right foot falls to the ground, left foot shovels leftward and crouches horizontally into left crouch stance. Meanwhile, left palm presses down to front of crotch by front of chest, with palm downward and fingers rightward; right palm turns over and parries above right side of the head, with palm up and palm fingers leftward. Eyes look leftward. (Figure 40, Attached figure 40)

Key points: turn body agilely; jump shall be light and step falls steadily, the whole action shall be coherent and consistent.

圖 41

23. 前掃腿　Sweep leg forward

（1）接上勢。重心左移成右仆步；同時，兩掌下落於襠前扶地；目視右腿。（圖 41 ）

（1）Follow the above posture, shift the barycenter leftward into right crouch stance. Meanwhile, both palms fall in front of crotch to support on floor. Eyes look at the right leg.（Figure 41 ）

圖 42

（2）上動不停。左轉身 180°，右腳以左腳為軸，向前、向左掃腿半周；同時，兩手隨身扶地於襠前；目視右腳。（圖 42）

要點：左腳掌碾地，右掃腿快速有力。

（2）Keep the above action, turn the body 180° to the left. Right foot sweeps half circle forward and leftward pivoting on left foot. Meanwhile, support with both hands in front of crotch. Eyes look at the right foot.（Figure 42）

Key points: grind floor with left sole; right sweeping leg shall be fast and forceful.

看家拳（一路）

圖 43

24. 騎馬勢　Horse‐riding posture

（1）接上勢。重心右移成馬步；同時，兩手變拳，屈肘合於胸前並齊，兩拳心均向裏，拳面均向上，高與肩平；目視前方。（圖 43）

（1）Follow the above posture, move the barycenter rightward into horse stance. Meanwhile, change both hands into fist, bend the elbows and fold in front of chest tidily, with both fist‐palms inward, fist‐planes up at the shoulders height. Eyes look forward.（Figure 43）

圖 44

（2）上動不停。兩拳自胸前分別向身體兩側平沖，兩拳眼均向前，拳心均向下，高與肩平；目視左方。（圖 44）

要點：同第 13 勢。

（2）Keep the above action, both fists thrust horizontally from front of chest to both sides of body, with both fist－holes forward and fist－palms down at the shoulders height. Eyes look leftward.（Figure 44）

Key points: the same as in Posture 13.

圖 45

25. 匡捶　Parry with hammer

（1）接上勢。左拳抱於腰間，拳心向上；同時，右
拳屈臂向下、向裏畫弧並向外格肘，拳心向裏，高與
眉齊；目視右拳。（圖 45）

(1) Follow the above posture, hold the left fist on the waist, with fist–palms up. Meanwhile, the right fist draws a circle downward and inward with the arm bent, and parry the right elbow outward, with fist–palms inward, in height of eyebrow. Eyes look at right fist.（Figure 45）

圖 46

(2) 上動不停。右拳收抱於腰間，拳心向上；同時，左拳從裏向外格肘，拳心向裏，高與眉齊；目視左拳。（圖 46）

(2) Keep the above action, draw back and hold the right fist on the waist, with fist−palm up. Meanwhile, parry the left elbow from inside to outside, with fist −palm inward in height of eyebrow. Eyes look at the left fist.（Figure 46）

圖 47

26. 弓步沖拳　Thrust fist in bow stance

接上勢。身體右轉 90°，重心前移成左弓步；同時，左拳抱於腰間，拳心向上；右拳向前平沖，拳眼向裏，拳面向前，高與肩平；目視前方。（圖 47）

要點：蹬腿擰腰抖肩沖拳，力達拳面。

Follow the above posture, turn the body 90° to the right, shift the barycenter forward into left bow stance. Meanwhile, hold the left fist on the waist, with fist–palm up; right fist thrusts horizontally forward, with fist –hole inward and fist –plane of the fist forward, at the shoulder height. Eyes look forward. 〔Figure 47〕

Key points: heel kick and twist waist, shake shoulder to punch the fist, with the force that shall reach the fist–face.

圖 48

27. 彈腿沖拳 Snap kick and thrust fist

(1) 接上勢。重心前移，左腿獨立，右腿抬起向前
彈踢，腳面繃直；同時，右拳抱於腰間，拳心向上；
左拳向前平沖，拳心向下，拳面向前，高與肩平；目
視前方。（圖 48）

(2) Follow the above posture, shift the barycenter for−ward
to stand on left leg, lift right leg to kick forward, with instep in
tight straightness. Meanwhile, right fist embraces in waist, with
fist−palm up; left fist thrusts horizontally forward, with fist−
palm down, fist−plane forward, at the shoulders height. Eyes
look forward. (Figure 48)

看家拳（一路）

圖 49

（2）上動不停。重心前移，右腳向前落地，左腿抬起向前彈踢，腳面繃直；同時，左拳抱於腰間，拳心向上；右拳向前平沖，拳心向下，拳面向前，高與肩平；目視前方。（圖 49）

(2) Keep the above action, shift the barycenter for-ward, right foot lands to the ground forward, left leg lifts to kick forward, with instep in tight straightness. Meanwhile, hold the left fist on the waist, with fist-palm up; right fist thrusts horizontally forward, with fist-palm down, fist-plane forward, at the shoulders height. Eyes look forward. (Figure 49)

圖 50

(3) 上動不停。重心前移，左腳向前落地，右腿抬起向前彈踢，腳面繃直；同時，右拳抱於腰間，拳心向上；左拳向前平沖，拳心向下，拳面向前，高與肩平；目視前方。（圖 50）

要點：上步彈踢與沖拳要協調一致，力達拳面和腳面，整個動作快速連貫。

看家拳（一路）

Figure 50

(3) Keep the above action, move the barycenter forward, left foot lands to the ground forward, right leg lifts to kick forward, with instep in tight straightness. Mean–while, hold the right fist on the waist, with fist –palm up; left fist thrusts horizontally forward, with fist–palm down, fist–plane of the fist forward, at the shoulders height. Eyes look forward. (Figure 50)

Key points: step on to snack kick and thrust fist shall be harmonic and consistent, with the force that shall reach striking surface of the fist and instep, the whole action shall be speedy and coherent.

圖 51

28. 翻身護肩掌
Turn over and guard shoulder with palm

(1) 接上勢。右腿屈膝，右腳不落地；同時，右臂下垂於體側，拳心向裏，拳面向下；左拳變掌抓拍右肩，掌指向後，虎口向裏；目視左手。（圖 51）

(1) Follow the above posture, bend the right knee and keep the right foot off floor. Meanwhile, the right arm drops at side of body, with fist–palm inward and fist–plane down; left fist changes into palm to grab and slap the right shoulder, with the finger backward, tiger's mouth inward. Eyes look at the left hand.（Figure 51）

圖 52

（2）上動不停。右腳外擺，身體右轉 180°，右膝隨身轉過，右腳不落地；同時，右臂屈肘，隨身外旋，肘尖向下，右拳面向上，拳心向裏；目視前方。（圖52）

（2）Keep the above action, swing outward right foot, turn body 180° to the right. The right knee turns with body, with right foot not landing on floor. Meanwhile, bend the right elbow to rotate the right arm outward with body, keep tip of elbow downward, fist－plane up, with fist－palm inward. Eyes look forward.（Figure 52）

看家拳（一路）套路動作圖解

圖 53

（3）上動不停。右腳震腳併步，身體下蹲成蹲步；
同時，右肘隨身下壓於胸前；目視前下方。（圖 53）

要點：轉身迅速，震腳有力，蹲步大腿接近水平，
周身合勁右肘下壓，力達肘尖。

(3) Keep the above action, stamp with the right foot, and
bring two feet together, squat down body into squat stance.
Meanwhile right elbow presses down in front of chest. Eyes look
downward ahead.〔Figure 53〕

Key points: turn body fast, stamp foot forcefully, squat
thigh near to horizontally, combine force around the body and
press down the right elbow, with force reaching the elbow tip.

圖 54

29. 金龍抱玉柱
Golden dragon embraces jade – column

（1）接上勢。重心稍上提；同時，右拳變掌，兩掌交叉並向上架掌於頭頂，兩掌心均向前，掌指斜向上；目視前方。（圖54、圖54附圖）

圖 54 附圖

(1) Follow the above posture, lift the barycenter slightly. Meanwhile, change the right fist into palm, cross the two palms and parry the palms upward above the head top. Keey both the palms forward, fingers inclining up. Eyes look forward. (Figure 54, Attached figure 54)

圖 55

(2) 上動不停。左腳向前上半步，右腳跟離地，重心落於右腳成跪步；同時，兩掌外分下落，然後在胸前交叉立掌，兩掌心均向外，掌指均向上；目視前方（圖 55）

(2) Keep the above action, the left foot takes a half – step forward, with the right heel off floor, and the barycenter shifts on right foot into kneel stance. Meanwhile, both palms depart outward to fall, then cross and stand the palms in front of chest, with both palms outward and fingers up. Eyes look forward. (Figure 55)

圖 56

30. 童子拜佛　The boy worships Buddha

（1）接上勢。兩腳蹬地向前跳起；同時，兩掌交叉上舉，再向身體兩側分掌，兩掌心均向外，掌指均向上，高與肩平；目視前方。（圖 56）

（1）Follow the above posture, the two feet step floor to jump forward. Meanwhile, both palms lift in crossing and depart at both sides of body, with both palms outward and fingers up, at the shoulders height. Eyes look forward.（Figure 56）

圖 57

　　(2) 上動不停。兩腳先後落地，左腳在前、右腳在後仍成跪步；同時，兩掌從身體兩側向胸前交叉立掌，兩掌心均向外，高與肩平；目視前方。（圖 57）

　　要點：雙腳跳步要遠，落地穩固，上下身密切配合。

　　(2) Keep the above action, the two feet land to the ground in order, left foot in front and right foot at back in kneel stance. Meanwhile, cross and stand both palms in front of chest from both sides of body, with both palms outward, at the shoulders height. Eyes look forward. (Figure 57)

　　Key points: both feet jump step shall be far, and fall on floor steadily, the upper and lower body cooperate closely.

圖 58

看家拳（一路）套路動作圖解

第三段　Section Three

31. 野馬分鬃　Part the wild horse's mane

(1) 接上勢。身體起立，略向右轉身；同時，左手向上挑掌；右掌隨身向上、向後撥掌，兩掌心均向外，掌指均向上，兩臂呈水平；目視右掌。（圖 58）

(1) Follow the above posture, stand up and turn body slightly right. Meanwhile, raise the left palm; move the right palm upward and backward with body, keep both palms outward and fingers upward, and the two arms in horizontal form. Eyes look at the right palm.（Figure 58）

圖 59

（2）上動不停。身體略向左轉，右腿屈膝獨立，左膝提起；同時，右掌隨身向前、向上挑掌於胸前，掌心向前；左掌隨身向上、向後撥掌，掌心向後，兩掌指均向上；目視右掌。（圖 59）

（2）Keep the above action, turn body slightly left. Stand on the right leg with the right knee bent, and lift the left knee. Meanwhile, raise the right palm forward and upward with body in front of the chest, with the palm forward; move the left palm upward and backward with body, keep the palm backward. Both palm fingers up. Eyes look at the right palm.（Figure 59）

圖 60

32. 八步趕蟬　Chase cicada in eight steps

（1）接上勢。身體略向右轉，左腳向前落步，右腳前掌向後搓地提起，腳跟接近臀部；同時，右掌隨身向上、向後撥掌，掌心向後；左手向前、向上挑掌，左臂微屈，掌心向前。兩掌指均向上；目視右掌。（圖 60）

Figure 60

(1) Follow the above posture, turn body right slightly. The left foot lands forward, the anterior sole of the right foot lifts through shuffling floor backward, with the heel near buttock Meanwhile, move the right palm upward and backward with body, and keep the palm backward; raise the left hand forward and upward, with the left arm slightly bent and the palm forward. Keep both palm fingers up. Eyes look at the right palm. (Figure 60)

圖61

　(2) 上動不停。身體略向左轉，右腳向前落步，左腳前掌向後搓地提起，腳跟接近臀部；同時，左掌隨身向上、向後撥掌，掌心向後；右手向前、向上挑掌，右臂微屈，掌心向前，兩掌指均向上；目視左掌。（圖61）

　(2) Keep the above action, turn body left slightly. The right foot lands forward, the anterior sole of the left foot lifts through shuffling floor backward, with the heel near buttock. Meanwhile, move the left palm upward and backward with body, with palm backward; raise the right palm forward and upward, with the right arm bent slightly and the palm forward. Keep both palm fingers up. Eyes look at the left palm.（Figure 61）

圖 62

（3）上動不停。身體略向右轉，左腳向前落步，右腳前掌向後搓地提起，腳跟接近臀部；同時，右掌隨身向上、向後撥掌，掌心向後；左手向前、向上挑掌，左臂微屈，掌心向前，兩掌指均向上；目視右掌。（圖62）

(3) Keep the above action, turn body right slightly. The left foot lands forward, anterior sole of the right foot lifts through shuffling floor backward, with the heel near buttock. Meanwhile, move the right palm upward and backward with body, and palm backward; raise the left hand forward and upward, with the left arm bent slightly and the palm forward. Keep both palm fingers up. Eyes look at the right palm.（Figure 62）

圖63

（4）上動不停。身體略向左轉，右腳向前落步，左腳前掌向後搓地提起，腳跟接近臀部；同時，左掌隨身向上、向後撥掌，掌心向後；右手向前、向上挑掌，右臂微屈，掌心向前，兩掌指均向上；目視左掌。（圖63）

（4）Keep the above action, turn body left slightly. The right foot falls forward, anterior sole of the left foot lifts through shuffling floor backward, with the heel near buttock. Meanwhile, move the left palm upward and backward with body, with the palm backward; raise the right hand forward and upward, with the right arm bent slightly and the palm forward. Keep both fingers up. Eyes look at the left palm.（Figure 63）

圖 64

　　(5) 上動不停。身體略向右轉，左腳向前落步，右腳前掌向後搓地提起，腳跟接近臀部；同時，右掌隨身向上、向後撥掌，掌心向後；左手向前、向上挑掌，左臂微屈，掌心向前，兩掌指均向上；目視右掌。（圖 64）

　　(5) Keep the above action, turn body right slightly. The left foot falls forward, anterior sole of the right foot lifts through shuffling the floor backward, with the heel near buttock. Meanwhile, move the right palm upward and backward with body, and palm backward; raise the left palm forward and upward, with the left arm bent slightly with the palm forward. Keep both palm fingers up. Eyes look at the right palm. (Figure 64)

看家拳（一路）套路動作圖解

圖 65

(6) 上動不停。身體略向左轉，右腳向前落步；同時，左掌擺至頭左上方，掌心向前，掌指向上；右掌落於右胯側，掌心向後，掌指向下；目視前方。（圖65）

要點：整個動作要連貫協調，步伐輕靈，節奏分明。

(6) Keep the above action, turn the body left slightly. The right foot falls forward. Meanwhile, swing the left palm above the left part of the head, with the palm forward and palm fingers up; the right palm falls at right side of hip, with the palm backward and palm fingers down. Eyes look forward.（Figure 65）

Key points: the whole action shall be coherent and consistent; the step shall be light and flexible, in clear rhythm.

圖 66

33. 二起腳　Jumping kick twice

（1）接上勢。右腿獨立，左膝提起；同時，右掌上擺於頭頂與左掌擊響，左掌在上，右掌在下，兩掌心均向下；目視前方。（圖66）

（1）Follow the above posture, stand on the right leg, and lift the left knee. Meanwhile, swing the right palm upward to top of head and slap with loud sound with the left palm. Keep the left palm above and right palm below, with both palms down. Eyes look forward.（Figure 66）

看家拳（一路）套路動作圖解

圖 67

（2）上動不停。右腿蹬地跳起向上彈踢；同時，左拳抱於腰間，拳心向上；右掌前伸，在空中拍擊右腳面；目視右腳。（圖 67）

要點：起跳要高，右掌擊響力點準確，聲音清脆。

（2）Keep the above action, press against the floor with the right leg to jump and snack kick upward. Meanwhile, hold the left fist on the waist, with the fist –palm up; the right palm extends forward to clap the right instep in the air. Eyes look at the right foot.（Figure 67）

Key points: jump must be high, slapping point of the right palm must be accurate with clear sound.

圖 68

34. 旋風腿　Whirlwind kick

（1）接上勢。身體左轉 90°，兩腳落地成馬步；同時，左拳隨身落於襠前，拳心向下，拳眼向裏；右掌變拳擺於身後，拳心向下，拳眼向外；目視左拳。（圖 68）

（1）Follow the above posture, turn the body 90° to the left. The two feet land to the ground in horse −riding stance. Meanwhile, the left fist lands in front of crotch with body, keep the fist −palm down and fist −hole inward; the right palm changes into fist to swing backward of body, with the fist−palm down and fist−hole outward. Eyes look at the left fist. (Figure 68)

圖 69

　(2) 上動不停。左腿提膝，隨即右腳蹬地跳起，身體騰空左轉 180°，在空中右腿裏合；同時，左掌向裏擊拍右腳掌。（圖 69）

　(2) Keep the above action, the left leg lifts knee, then the right foot steps on floor to jump instantly, the body jumps to turn left by 180° in the air. Swing the right leg inward in the air. （Figure 69）

圖 70

　（3）上動不停。身體繼續左轉 180°，雙腳落地站立；同時，右掌落於身前，掌心向下，掌指向前；左掌擺於左胯側，掌心向裏，掌指向下；目視右掌。（圖 70）

　　要點：同第 12 式。

　（3）Keep the above action, the body continues to turn left by 180°, both feet land on the ground to stand. Meanwhile, the right palm falls in front of the body, with palm down and fingers forward; swing the left palm at left side of hip, with palm inward and fingers down. Eyes look at the right palm.（Figure 70）

　　Key points: the same as that of Form 12.

圖 71

35. 代腿飛擺蓮
Flying lotus kick with additional leg

(1) 接上勢。身體右轉 90°，左腳屈膝向後擺踢接近臀部；同時，左掌隨身上擺於頭左上方，掌心向上，掌指向右；右掌向後擊拍左腳內側；目視右掌。（圖 71）

(1) Follow the above posture, turn the body 90° to the right. Bend the left knee to swing and kick the left foot backward near to buttock. Meanwhile, swing the left palm upward above the left part of head, with the palm up and fingers rightward; right palm slaps the inner side of the left foot backward. Eyes look at the right palm.（Figure 71）

圖72

（2）上動不停。右腳尖外擺，身體繼續右轉90°；同時，左掌向下擊拍左腳外側；右掌上擺於頭右上方，掌心向前，掌指向左；目視左掌。（圖72）

（2）Keep the above action, turn the right tiptoe out–ward, and the body continues to turn right by 90°. Meanwhile, the left palm slaps the outer side of left foot downward; swing the right palm upward above the right part of head, with the palm forward and fingers leftward. Eyes look at the left palm.（Figure 72）

圖 73

（3）上動不停。右腳蹬地跳起並向右做外擺腿，身體騰空右轉 180°；同時，兩掌面前依次擊拍右腳背；目視右腳。（圖 73）

要點：外擺蓮騰空要高，迅速有力。

(3) Keep the above action, the right foot steps on floor to jump and swing outward to the right. The body jumps to turn 180° to the right. Meanwhile, both palms slap the right instep in turn. Eyes look at the right foot.（Figure 73）

Key points: outward lotus leg swing jump shall be high, speedy and forceful.

圖74

36. 洪門射雁
Shoot wild goose at Hongmen

（1）接上勢。左腳下落，右腳外擺落地，身體下蹲成馬步；同時，左掌收於腰間，掌心向上，掌指向前；右掌向下畫掌並向裏摟手，掌心向下，掌指向左置於身前；目視右掌。（圖74）

看家拳（一路）套路動作圖解

(1) Follow the above posture, the left foot lands to the ground, the right foot swings outward and lands to the ground, the body squats into horse stance. Meanwhile, draw back the left palm on the waist, with the palm up and fingers forward; swing the right palm downward, grab it inward, and place it in front of the body, with the palm down and fingers leftward. Eyes look at the right palm. (Figure 74)

看家拳（一路）

圖 75

(2) 上動不停。身體略向右轉成右弓步；同時，右掌摟抓變拳抱於腰間，拳心向上；左掌向左平推掌，掌心向外，掌指向上；目視左方。（圖 75）

(2) Keep the above action, the body turns slightly to the right into right bow stance. Meanwhile, grab the right palm into fist and hold the right fist on the waist, with the fist – palm up; left palm pushes horizontally to the left, with the palm outward and fingers up. Eyes look leftward.（Figure 75）

圖 76

37. 左右梅花手
Left and right plumb – blossom hand

（1）接上勢。身體微向左轉，起立；同時，左掌隨身向上、向左畫掌，置於身左側；右拳變掌，向前、向上擺掌，兩掌指均向外，掌心均向下；目視前方。（圖 76）

（1）Follow the above posture, turn the body left slightly and stand up. Meanwhile, swing the left palm up – ward and leftward with body, and put it at the left side of body; change the right fist into palm and swing the palm forward and upward, with both fingers outward and palm down. Eyes look forward.（Figure 76）

圖77

(2)上動不停。右腳向右前方上半步，身體下蹲成右虛步；同時，左掌翻掌成掌心向上並畫掌於右膝上方；右掌由外向裏畫掌，與左掌交叉於胸前，掌心向下，掌指向左下方；目視左掌。（圖77）

(2) Keep the above action, the right foot steps a half – step right forward, and the body squats down into right empty stance. Meanwhile, the left palm turns over into the palm upward, and swing the palm above the right knee; swing the right palm from outward to inward, and cross it with the left palm in front of chest, with the palm down and fingers left downward. Eyes look at the left palm.（Figure 77）

看家拳（一路）套路動作圖解

圖78

（3）上動不停。右腳向右後方退半步，身體起立；同時，右掌走上弧向外畫掌；左掌走下弧向外畫掌，兩掌心均向下，掌指均向外；目視前方。（圖78）

（3）Keep the above action, the right foot steps a half–step right backward, stand up. Meanwhile, the right palm swings upper circle outward; the left palm swings lower circle outward. Keep both palms downward, and fingers outward. Eyes look forward.〔Figure 78〕

圖 79

(4) 上動不停。左腳向左前方上半步，身體下蹲成左虛步；同時，右掌翻掌成掌心向上並畫掌於左膝上方；左掌由外向裏畫掌，與右掌交叉於胸前，掌心向下，掌指向右下方；目視右掌。（圖 79）

要點：整個動作要輕靈敏捷，快速連貫。

(4) Keep the above action, the left foot takes a half–step left –ward, the body squats down into left empty stance Meanwhile, turn over right palm into its center upward and swing the palm above the left knee; swing the left palm from outward to inward, and cross it with the right palm in front of chest, with the palm down and fingers right downward. Eyes look at the right palm.（Figure 79）

Key points: the whole action shall be light and agile, speedy and consistent.

看家拳（一路）

圖 80

38. 虛步亮掌

Flash palm in empty stance

接上勢。左掌向外、向後擺掌，變鉤手置於左臀後方，鉤尖向上；同時，右掌向外、向上架掌於頭前上方，掌心向上，掌指向左；目視左方。（圖 80）

Follow the above posture, swing the left palm outward and backward, change it into hook hand and put it in back of left crotch, with the hook tip up. Meanwhile, parry with the right palm outward and upward to front top of head, with the palm up and fingers leftward. Eyes look leftward. (Figure 80)

圖81

39. 謝步請勢
Invitation posture with backward step

（1）接上勢。左腳向左後方退一步；同時，左鉤手變掌，並向前、向上穿掌，掌心向右，掌指向前，高與肩平；右掌翻腕，經胸前畫掌於左腋下，掌心向上，掌指向左；目視左掌。（圖81）

Figure 81

(1) Follow the above posture, the left foot withdraws one step left backward. Meanwhilem, change the left hook hand into palm and thread the palm forward and upward, with the palm rightward and fingers forward, at the shoulders height; the right palm turns wrist to swing palm below left armpit by front of chest, with the palm up and fingers leftward. Eyes look at the left palm. (Figure 81)

圖 82

（2）上動不停。重心後移，右腳向右後方退一步；
同時，左掌向上、向外擺掌於左前方，掌心向外，掌
指向上，高與肩平；右掌走下弧向右後方擺掌，掌心
斜向上，掌指向外，兩臂呈一直線；目視右掌。（圖
82）

（2）Keep the above action, move the barycenter backward,
and the right foot withdraws a step right backward. Meanwhile,
swing the left palm upward and outward to left front side, with
the palm outward and fingers upward, at the shoulders height;
the right palm swings lower circle to right backward, with the
palm up aslant and fingers outward. Keep the two arms in line.
Eyes look at the right palm.（Figure 82）

圖 83

（3）上動不停。左腳向右腳併步，身體直立；同時，左手向下、向裏畫掌抱於腹前，掌心向上，掌指向右；右手向外、向上擺掌於頭前上方，掌心向上，掌指向左；目視前方。（圖 83）

　　要點：兩手動作要與退步協調一致。

(3) Keep the above action, bring the left foot to the right one, stand upright. Meanwhile, swing the left palm downward and inward and hold it in front of abdomen, with the palm up and fingers rightward; swing the right palm outward and upward to top front of head, with the palm up and fingers leftward. Eyes look forward.（Figure 83）

Key points: actions of both hands shall be in harmony and consistent with stepping backward.

圖 84

40. 收勢　Closing form

（1）接上勢。右腳向右後方退一步，身體微向右轉；同時，右掌經胸前向下按掌，然後兩掌分別從身體兩側上托於頭兩側上方，兩掌心相對，掌指斜向上；目視右掌。（圖 84）

（1）Follow the above posture, the right foot withdraws one step right backward. Turn body slightly turns right. Meanwhile, press the right palm down by front of chest, then raise both palms above both sides of head from both sides of the body, with both palms opposite and fingers upward aslant. Eyes look at the right palm.（Figure 84）

圖 85

(2) 上動不停。身體微左轉，左腳向右腳併步；同時，兩掌經胸前下按於兩胯側，兩掌心均向下，掌指均向前；目視前方。（圖 85）

(2) Keep the above action, turn the body slightly left. Bring the left foot to the right one. Meanwhile, press both palms down at both sides of hips by front of chest, with both palms down and fingers forward. Eyes look forward.〔Figure 85〕

圖 86

(3) 上動不停。兩掌同時自然下垂至身體兩側；目視前方。（圖 86）

要點：挺胸收腹，平心靜氣，體態自然，精神內斂。

(3) Keep the above action, both palms hang to both sides of body naturally simultaneously. Eyes look forward.（Figure 86）

Key points: lift the chest and draw in the abdomen, be calm in natural posture, and collect the vital energy inward.

看家拳（一路）

全套動作演示圖

Demonstration of All the Action

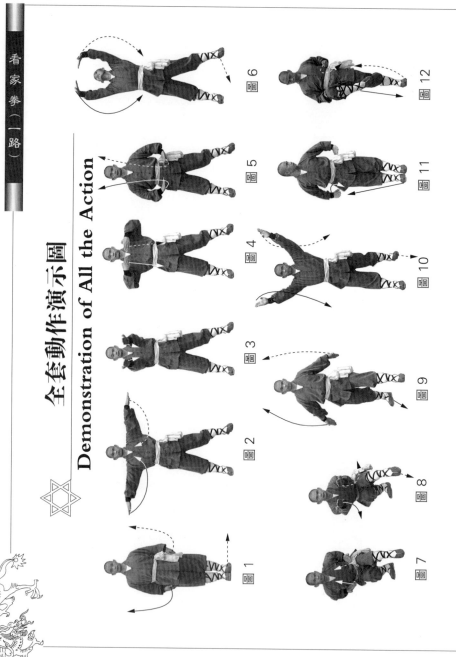

图1

图2

图3

图4

图5

图6

图7

图8

图9

图10

图11

图12

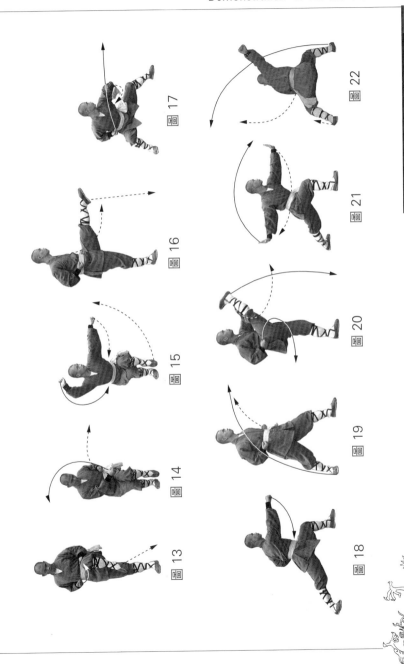

看家拳（一路）

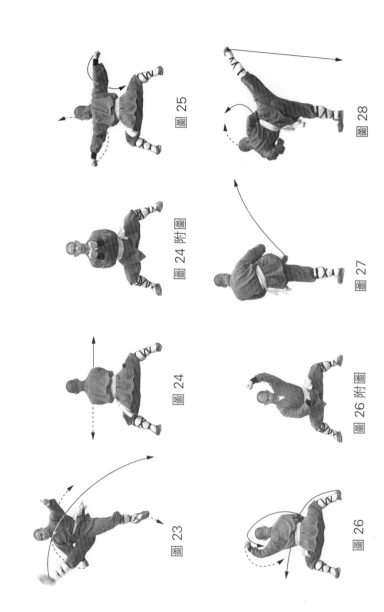

圖 25

圖 24 附

圖 24

圖 23

圖 28

圖 27

圖 26 附

圖 26

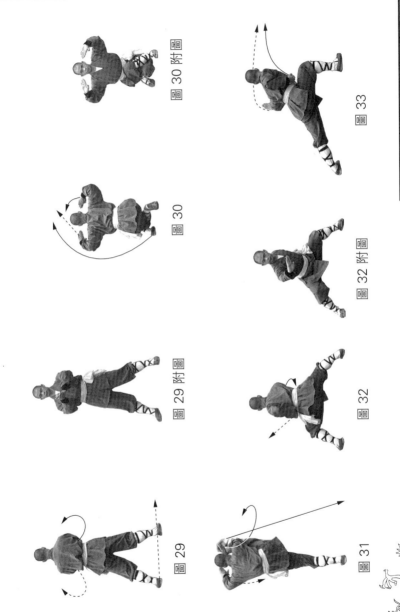

全套動作演示圖

圖 30 附圖

圖 30

圖 29 附圖

圖 29

圖 33

圖 32 附圖

圖 32

圖 31

看家拳（一路）

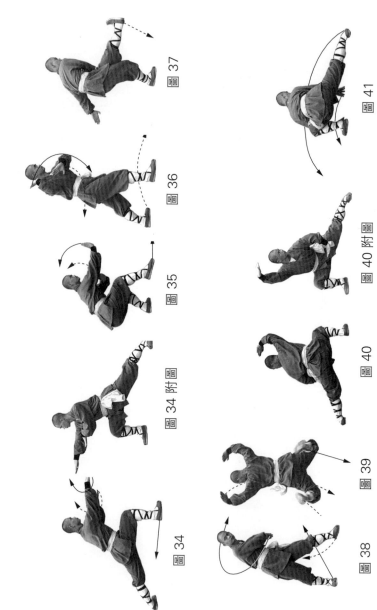

图 37

图 36

图 35

图 34 附图

图 34

图 41

图 40 附图

图 40

图 39

图 38

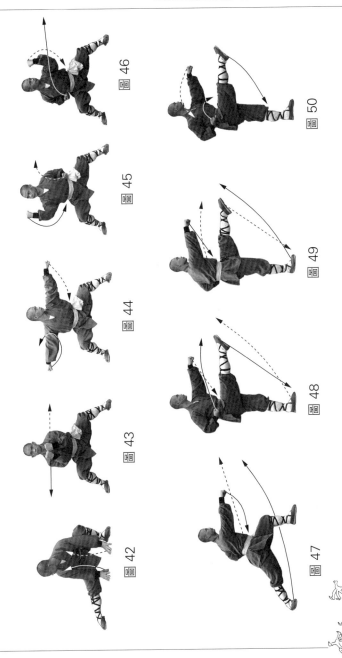

全套動作演示圖

看家拳（一路）

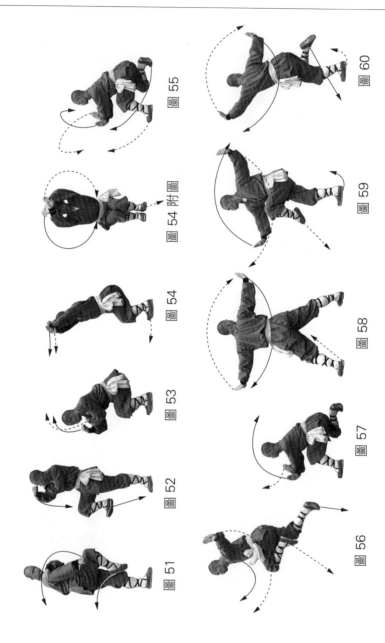

圖 55

圖 54 附

圖 54

圖 53

圖 52

圖 51

圖 60

圖 59

圖 58

圖 57

圖 56

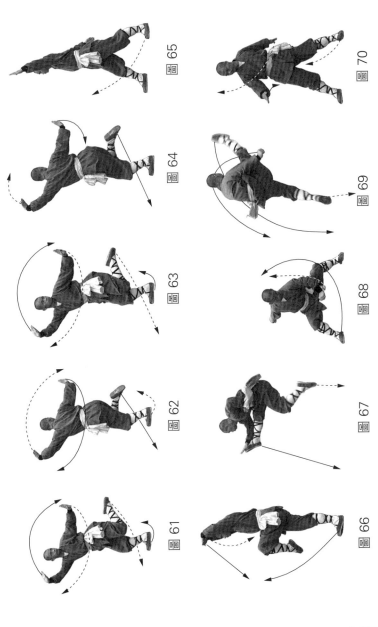

全套動作演示圖

看家拳（一路）

圖 75

圖 74

圖 73

圖 72

圖 71

圖 80

圖 79

圖 78

圖 77

圖 76

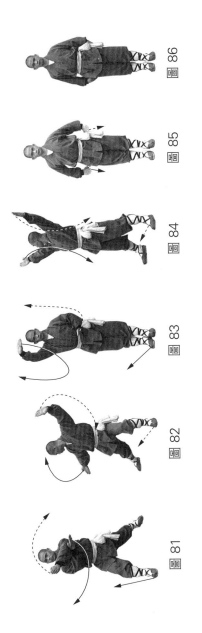

全套動作演示圖

國家圖書館出版品預行編目資料

看家拳（一路）／耿　軍　著
　　　──初版，──臺北市，大展，2008〔民97.04〕
　　　面；21 公分 ──（少林傳統功夫漢英對照系列；11）
　　　ISBN　978－957－468－603－2（平裝）

1.少林拳　2.中國
528.972　　　　　　　　　　　　　　　　　97002699

看 家 拳（一路）

ISBN　978－957－468－603－2

著　　者／耿　軍
責任編輯／朱　曉　峰
發 行 人／蔡　森　明
出 版 者／大展出版社有限公司
社　　址／台北市北投區（石牌）致遠一路2段12巷1號
電　　話／（02）28236031・28236033・28233123
傳　　眞／（02）28272069
郵政劃撥／01669551
網　　址／www.dah-jaan.com.tw
E - mail ／ service@dah-jaan.com.tw
登 記 證／局版臺業字第2171號
承 印 者／傳興印刷有限公司
裝　　訂／建鑫裝訂有限公司
排 版 者／弘益電腦排版有限公司
授 權 者／北京人民體育出版社
初版1刷／2008年（民97年）4月

定　價／180元

推理文學經典巨著，中文版正式授權

名偵探明智小五郎與怪盜的挑戰與鬥智
名偵探柯南、金田一都讚嘆不已

日本推理小說鼻祖—江戶川亂步

1894年10月21日出生於日本三重縣名張〈現在的名張市〉。本名平井太郎。
就讀於早稻田大學時就曾經閱讀許多英、美的推理小說。
畢業之後曾經任職於貿易公司，也曾經擔任舊書商、新聞記者等各種工作。
1923年4月，在『新青年』中發表「二錢銅幣」。
筆名江戶川亂步是根據推理小說的始祖艾德嘉·亞藍波而取的。
後來致力於創作許多推理小說。
1936年配合「少年俱樂部」的要求所寫的『怪盜二十面相』極受人歡迎，
陸續發表『少年偵探團』、『妖怪博士』共26集……等
適合少年、少女閱讀的作品。

1～3集　定價300元　試閱特價189元